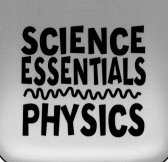

SCIENCE ESSENTIALS
PHYSICS

Light and Colours

GERARD CHESHIRE

EVANS

EVANS
LONDON

© Evans Brothers Ltd 2006

Published by:
Evans Brothers
2a Portman Mansions
Chiltern Street
London W1U 6NR

Series editor:
Harriet Brown

Editor:
Harriet Brown

Design:
Simon Morse

Illustrations:
Q2A Creative

Printed in China by
WKT Company Limited

British Library Cataloguing in
Publication Data

 Cheshire, Gerard, 1965-
   Light and colour. - (Science
essentials. Physics)
   1.Light - Juvenile literature 2.Color
- Juvenile literature
   I.Title
   535

ISBN-10: 0237530058
13-digit ISBN (from 1 January 2007)
978 0 23753005 1

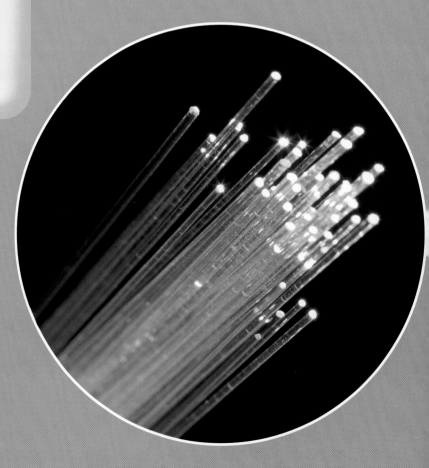

Contents

Introduction

Light and colours affect our lives in a surprising number of ways. Not only do we need light to see, it allows plants to grow, makes telephones and CD

players work and can even affect our moods. Colours help us to decide whether food is safe to eat, they allow animals to hide in their natural environment and they supply us with messages every day.

In this book we take a closer look at light, what it is, where it comes from and how it travels. Find out how light is produced, learn all about the colours hidden in light and discover how light behaves when it meets an object. You can also find out how we see a world of colour, how we capture moments in time and how light and colour may be used to learn about life on Mars in the future.

This book contains feature boxes that will help you to unravel more about the mysteries of light and colours. Test yourself on what you have learnt so far; investigate some of the concepts discussed; find out more key facts; discover some of the scientific findings of the past and see how these might be utilised in the future.

DID YOU KNOW?

▶ Watch out for these boxes – they contain surprising and fascinating facts about light and colours.

TEST YOURSELF

▶ Use these boxes to see how much you've learnt. Try to answer the questions without looking at the book, but take a look if you are really stuck.

INVESTIGATE

▶ These boxes contain experiments that you can carry out at home. The equipment you will need is usually cheap and easy to find around the home.

TIME TRAVEL

▶ These boxes describe scientific discoveries from the past and fascinating developments that pave the way for the advance of science in the future.

ANSWERS

At the end of this book on pages 46 and 47, you will find the answers to the questions from the 'Test yourself' and 'Investigate' boxes.

GLOSSARY

Words highlighted in **bold** are described in detail in the glossary on pages 46 and 47.

What is light?

We take light for granted every day of our lives. Without light we would see nothing at all, no plants would grow and, because plants provide us with oxygen, there would not be enough oxygen to keep us alive. Our planet would be a dead and empty place. Scientists have shown that light is unlike anything else in the Universe. Nothing travels faster than light. But what is light?

LIGHT EXPLAINED

Light is a type of **radiation**. Radiation is energy that comes from a source, such as the Sun or a light bulb. Light travels as waves. The most important point about light travel is that the overall direction is always a straight line. So, light waves travel in a straight line until they are interrupted by an object.

For example, if two people each hold the end of a rope and one person quickly moves his end of the rope up and down, a wave travels along the rope. Even though the rope is bending, the progress of the wave is still a straight line from one person to the other. This is how light travels.

LIGHT DIRECTION

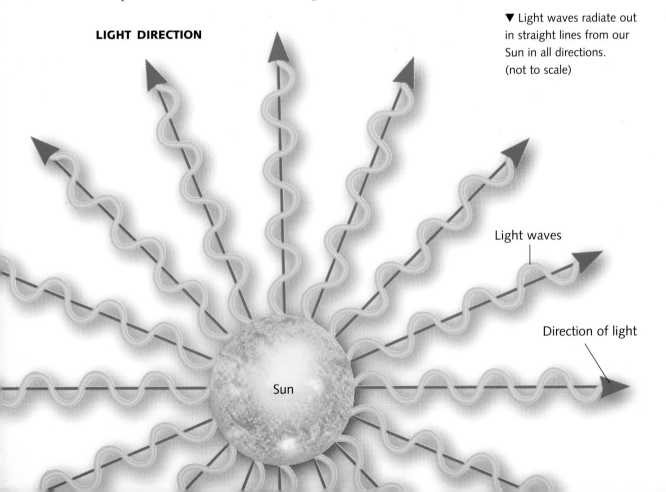

▼ Light waves radiate out in straight lines from our Sun in all directions. (not to scale)

Light waves

Direction of light

Sun

SHADOWS

Light cannot travel through **opaque** objects, such as people, and it cannot travel around corners. When an opaque object is put in the path of a light bulb, it blocks the light and creates a shadow.

SHADOW CASTING

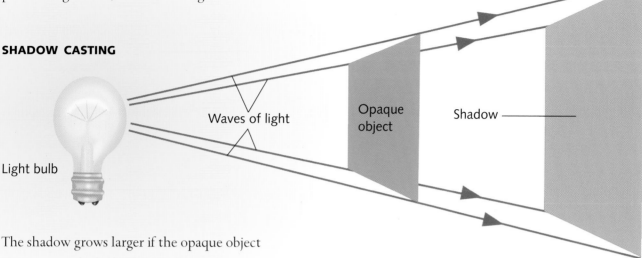

The shadow grows larger if the opaque object moves towards the light bulb. The light waves radiate out in straight lines from a single source, like the spokes of a wheel. The closer the object is to the bulb, the more light waves are blocked.

SHADOWS AND THE SUN

The shapes of shadows caused by sunlight change according to the angle of the Sun above the Earth. When the Sun is overhead, the light waves hit the top of an object, such as your head or a tree, and form a short, or round, shadow on the ground. When the Sun is setting, the light waves hit the object from side on and the shadow lengthens out along the ground.

▲ ▼ Light waves travel in straight lines. A shadow forms behind anything that gets in their way.

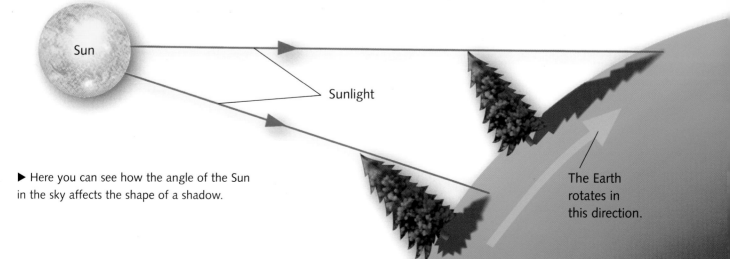

▶ Here you can see how the angle of the Sun in the sky affects the shape of a shadow.

TYPES OF SHADOW

Near objects give a sharp-edged shadow. This type of shadow is called an umbra and totally blocks the light. Far objects usually give a fuzzy-edged shadow. This type of shadow is called a pre-umbra and is also produced when the light comes from more than one point. Fuzzy shadows are very useful in situations such as schools and offices, where we need gradual changes in lighting – you wouldn't want half of your desk in shade and the other half in bright light.

At any time of day, half of planet Earth is in light and half is in shade. The part of our planet that is experiencing 'night time' is not receiving any direct sunlight and is in the Earth's shadow. One particular type of shadow experienced on Earth is an **eclipse**. Eclipses happen when the Moon is positioned in a line between the Earth and the Sun. The Moon temporarily casts a shadow over the Earth. Each year there are between two and three solar eclipses. They can be very confusing for wildlife; some creatures prepare to sleep for the night, only to be woken by daylight a few minutes later.

▲ At any time, half of the world is experiencing night time, and half is experiencing day time. Here you can see the border between night and day over western Europe and Africa.

INVESTIGATE

▶ A solar eclipse happens when the Moon is positioned between the Earth and the Sun. Use the library or the internet to find out what happens during a lunar eclipse. Write a short explanation of a lunar eclipse.
▶ Find out why it is very dangerous to look directly at the Sun, even during a solar eclipse.

COLOURS OF LIGHT

Light from the Sun (natural light) or a light bulb (artificial light), is called 'white light' because it appears to be white or a very pale yellow. However, white light is actually a mixture of different colours. Traditionally, there are seven colours of the rainbow – red, orange, yellow, green, blue, indigo and violet – which mix together to make white light. Scientifically, there are six colours in the rainbow as indigo is simply a variation of violet. We can see the separate colours of white light when we shine it through a prism or through droplets of water, as with a rainbow. A second prism can make the colours of light rejoin and become white light. Isaac Newton was the first person to demonstrate this in 1675.

Each colour of light has its own **wavelength**. A wavelength is a measure of the size of a wave and the colour that you see depends on the wavelength. Red light waves are longer than blue light waves, for example. White light, such as that in a lamp in your home, contains all the different wavelengths, and so contains all the colours of light.

▲ White light is split by a prism into the colours of the rainbow.

An easy way to remember the seven colours of the rainbow is

Richard **O**f **Y**ork **G**ave **B**attle **I**n **V**ain

WAVELENGTHS OF VISIBLE LIGHT

▶ Wavelengths are measured from the top of one wave to the top of the next. From red to violet, the wavelengths of the colours of the rainbow become shorter.

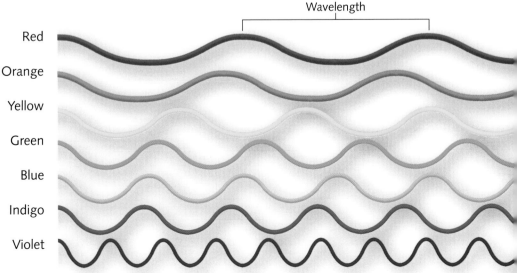

Red
Orange
Yellow
Green
Blue
Indigo
Violet

Wavelength

LIGHT SPEED

Scientists used to think that light travelled instantly, but today we know that this isn't the case. When we switch on a light bulb there is a delay between the light bulb sending out its light waves and the light flooding the room, but our brains are far too slow to notice. However, light travels extremely fast.

The **speed of light** is around 300,000 kilometres per second. It takes light from the Sun eight minutes to reach Earth. Light from the nearest bright star, Proxima Centauri, takes over four years to get here. A 'light year' might sound as though it is a measure of time, but in fact it is a measure of distance. It is the distance light travels in one year, which is a very long way indeed – 9,460,700,000,000 kilometres. Light can only travel this fast through space because it is a vacuum (a space containing nothing at all).

▼ When we look into the night sky, the light from some of the stars that we see has taken hundreds of years to travel to Earth.

Light slows down when it passes through **transparent** materials. In the case of air, water and glass, it makes little difference, but other transparent materials can have a dramatic effect. Some crystals slow light down to only tens of metres per second, but only in certain laboratory conditions. Reducing the strength of light is not the same as slowing it down. Tinted glass in a car window, for example, does not slow the light down but prevents some of the light from getting through.

FASTER THAN THE SPEED OF LIGHT?

Some scientists have suggested that there may actually be something faster than light, but it hasn't yet been discovered. They have even invented the name 'tachyon', which comes from the Greek for 'swift'. The tachyon, if it exists, will have no **mass** and will travel at infinite speed. In other words, it could travel from one end of the Universe to the other in an instant – which makes the speed of light seem rather slow. If the tachyon is ever found, it could have an incredible effect on communication technology.

▼ The tinted glass in sunglasses prevents some of the light from travelling to our eyes.

◀ Science fiction is full of references to vehicles that can travel at the speed of light. However, even at the speed of light, it would still take 100,000 years to travel from one side of our galaxy to the other.

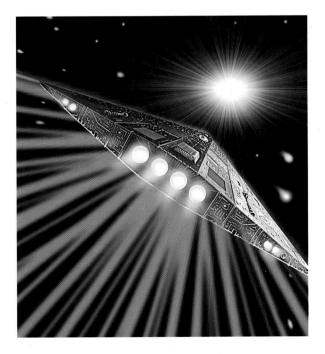

Types of light

For light to exist at all it has to come from somewhere – a light source. At night when our main light source, the Sun, is out of view, we rely on light produced by electricity. Before homes were powered by electricity, people burned gas, oil, candles, coal and wood to light their homes. But light can come from more unusual places, too. Some animals, including various fish and insects, produce their own light to communicate with other creatures. Powerful and concentrated light sources – lasers – are used for more than just lighting our world.

INCANDESCENT AND LUMINESCENT

There are two main types of light – **incandescent** and **luminescent**. Incandescent light is also called 'warm light', because it comes from things that give off light when they are very hot. The Sun, light bulbs and candles are incandescent light sources. Luminescent light is often called 'cold light', because it is not the result of burning or heating. Instead, cold light is produced by chemical reactions.

Your home is likely to be lit by ordinary light bulbs, which are incandescent light sources. The part of the light bulb that glows is called the filament and is made of a metal called tungsten. It becomes 'white hot' when it is heated by the electricity passing through it. Gases surround the filament and prevent it from burning out. This helps the bulb last as long as possible, usually up to 1,000 hours.

Fluorescent lights are luminescent light sources. Fluorescent light bulbs don't have a filament and they don't get hot. Gas inside the tube carries electricity, which causes a chemical coating on the inside of the glass to glow. They require relatively little electricity to run and they last a very long time – around 10,000 hours. They are also called energy-saving light bulbs.

▲ The filament of a light bulb glows white hot. It is an incandescent light source.

▲ This train is lit by fluorescent light bulbs. They are luminescent light sources.

ANIMALS AND LIGHT

When luminescent light comes from animals and plants, it is called **bioluminescence**. The main chemical is called 'luciferan', which creates light when it reacts with another chemical called 'luciferase'. Both chemicals get their name from 'Lucifer', which is another name for the devil, as bioluminescence is only seen in darkness when, according to certain religions, the devil is supposed to appear.

Bioluminescence is most frequently seen in ocean creatures such as fish, squid and plankton. It is also seen in glow worms and fire flies, as well as some fungi and bacteria. Organisms emit light for a variety of reasons. Some send out coded messages to attract a mate; others use light to attract prey.

In the oceans, creatures such as squid use bioluminescence to protect themselves from predators. When predators look for prey, they tend to look upwards, and search for a shadow or a silhouette. If the prey uses bioluminescence to match the light shining down from the Sun or Moon, it makes itself almost invisible from below.

▲ This adult female glow worm uses bioluminescence to attract a male.

Some fish have their own night vision. For example, the Malacosteid family of fishes (also called Loosejaws) produce red light and have the ability to see red light. Most ocean creatures can not see red light. This gives the fish a huge advantage over its prey – the fish can see and catch prey while remaining completely undetected.

Tiny creatures called dinoflagellates also use bioluminescence for protection. When they are disturbed by a predator, they flash. The flash attracts a secondary predator, such as a small fish. The fish is more likely to find and eat the first predator than the tiny dinoflagellate. Therefore, the predators of the dinoflagellate are removed.

◄ Dinoflagellates flash with light when anything physically disturbs the water, including the boat at the top of this photograph.

GLOW IN THE DARK

Glow-in-the-dark materials have many uses, such as in escape route lighting and on fire safety signs, but they are most commonly seen in toys. Glow-in-the-dark products must be held near a light source, such as a torch or lamp, to charge them up. Once this has been done the material will glow for several minutes, or many hours with some recently developed glow-in-the-dark paint. All glow-in-the-dark items contain phosphors. Phosphors are chemicals that absorb energy from a light source and then glow as they release the energy. This kind of light is called **phosphorescence**.

▲ Phosphorescent paint is often used to illuminate toys.

LASERS

Lasers are used in all sorts of places – inside CD players, as checkout scanners, in medical surgery, and for shaping diamonds. Laser light can be created when a flashlamp, like that found in a camera, flashes at a material such as a ruby. The flashlamp's energy makes the ruby atoms jump about and give out light. The light is channelled through a half-silvered mirror to produce laser light. Using a ruby gives out red laser light. To obtain different types or colours of lasers, the ruby is swapped for other materials such as alexandrite crystal.

White light is made of a mixture of colours (see page 9) and the light waves fan out from the light source. Laser light is different because it is all one colour and the waves do not fan out. The peaks and troughs of laser light waves are exactly lined up. This is called **coherence**. Laser light is called coherent light and ordinary white light is called incoherent light.

▶ Normal light contains all the colours of the rainbow, which all have different wavelengths. Laser light waves all have the same wavelength and do not fan out from the source.

Normal light

Laser light

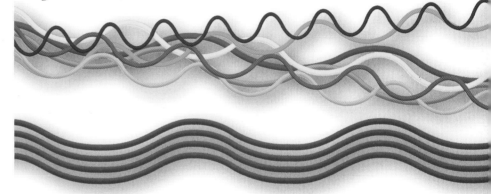

Lasers are more powerful than ordinary light. In surgery, laser beam scalpels are used for delicate operations. The heat from the laser seals tiny blood vessels as it cuts through the skin or tissue, which causes far less bleeding than using a normal scalpel. Laser beam scalpels are also sterile and reduce the chance of infection in the patient.

▼ The laser coming from this device is being used to repair damaged heart muscle.

Because laser beams form a precisely straight line, they are also used as measuring tools. In the construction industry, lasers are used to check whether buildings are absolutely straight. Lasers can measure distances, too. A beam is sent off, it bounces off a mirror and returns to its start point. To calculate the distance to the mirror and back, all you do is measure the time it takes and multiply it by the speed of light. Lasers are even used to measure changes in the Earth's surface. They can detect the change in mountain height and the position of continents, which only shift by a few centimetres a year.

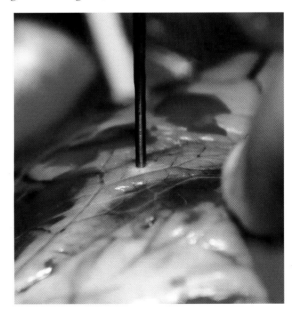

Reflection and refraction

Light waves travel in straight lines until something crosses their path. Some materials **reflect** (bounce) light waves very well, such as road signs and the reflective strips on trainers. Other objects bend light waves and change their direction. Light waves refract (change direction) when they hit the surface of water. This can deceive the eye into thinking that the bottom of a swimming pool or the bottom of a glass of water is closer than it really is.

REFLECTION

We would see nothing if it weren't for reflection. Everything we see reflects light towards our eyes. This is how the world is visible to us. For anything to reflect light, there needs to be a light source. Imagine you are in a very dark room at night and this book is on a desk. You would not be able to see it. If a lamp is switched on, you see the book because it reflects light from the lamp. The book is **non-luminous** and the lamp is **luminous**.

The differences in the way that light is reflected allows us to tell things apart, and build a picture of the world around us. The texture of a surface affects the way it reflects light. Most objects have a rough surface that scatters light in many directions. For example, a wooden table top and a piece of paper scatter light and appear dull. Any light that is not scattered is absorbed (soaked up).

The most reflective surfaces are mirrors. They have an extremely smooth and flat surface, and reflect nearly all of the light waves that hit them. This is why you see a near perfect reflection of yourself when you look in a mirror.

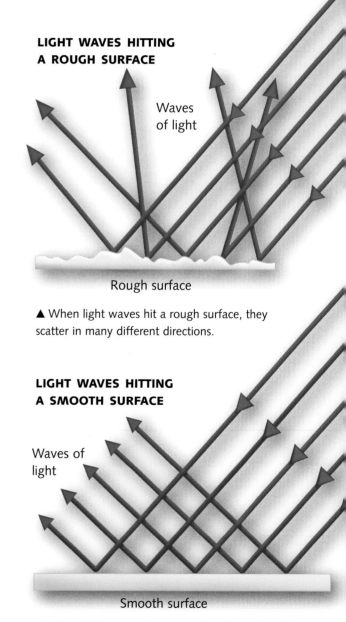

LIGHT WAVES HITTING A ROUGH SURFACE

Waves of light

Rough surface

▲ When light waves hit a rough surface, they scatter in many different directions.

LIGHT WAVES HITTING A SMOOTH SURFACE

Waves of light

Smooth surface

▲ When light waves hit a smooth surface, they all bounce off in the same direction.

Mirrors that are not completely flat can distort the mirror image by bouncing light waves in unexpected directions. Fun circus mirrors use this principle to make your mirror image look tall and skinny, or short, round and lumpy depending on how the mirror is curved. Curved mirrors can be used to collect and focus light, as in a telescope (see page 33).

◄ Mirrors or shiny windows that are not completely flat will distort the mirror image.

REFLECTION AND ANGLES

The light ray travelling to the surface of a mirror is called the incident ray. The light ray reflected by the mirror is called the reflected ray. A line drawn at a right angle (90 degrees) to the mirror is called the normal. The angle between the incident ray and the normal is the angle of incidence. The angle between the reflected ray and the normal is the angle of reflection. These two angles are always the same. Periscopes use the predictable behaviour of flat mirrors to bounce images between two mirrors and the eye, to help people see over tall objects.

Angle of incidence = angle of reflection
Angle i = angle r

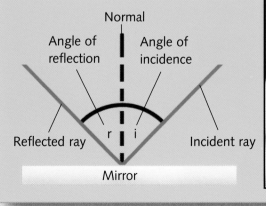

Normal

Angle of reflection   Angle of incidence

Reflected ray   r | i   Incident ray

Mirror

▼ Periscopes help sailors to see outside a submarine. Periscopes use mirrors to bounce the image to our eyes.

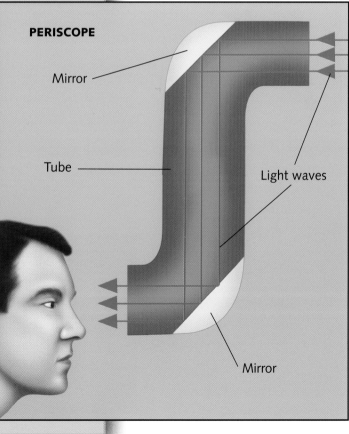

PERISCOPE

Mirror

Tube

Light waves

Mirror

CLEAR AND CLOUDY

Light passes easily through 'transparent' materials. When materials only allow some light through, they are called '**translucent**'. Frosted glass in a bathroom window is translucent. Frosted glass and translucent plastic are often used for lamp shades because they spread light from the bulb evenly across the room. This is called '**diffusion**'. If materials block light totally, they are described as 'opaque'.

REFRACTION

When light travels from one transparent substance to another, such as from air into water, the light waves change direction. This is refraction. Glass and water refract light. For example, a spoon standing in a glass of water looks bent or broken at the point where it meets the water. The light waves are slowed down by the water and change direction. Therefore, the image we see looks distorted.

Refraction can cause white light to divide into its different colours, so that we see a spectrum of colours. Scientists use glass prisms to experiment with refraction, but other pieces of cut glass produce the same effect – such as pieces of cut

INVESTIGATE

▶ We are all familiar with using mirrors to see reflections of our faces, but what about using mirrors to see our side profiles or the backs of our heads? How many mirrors does it take to see the back of your head?

▼ The water refracts light and makes the thermometer look bent.

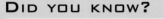

DID YOU KNOW?

▶ Myth has it that there is a pot of gold at the end of the rainbow. This idea arose because it is impossible to reach the end of a rainbow. The reason is that a rainbow is an optical illusion caused by refraction, rather than a physical object, so it appears to move farther away when it is chased.

crystal or the droplets from chandeliers. Rainbows, the mother-of-pearl effect seen on some sea shells, the colours on the surface of oil, and the **iridescent** colours of some insects are all caused by refraction. But how does it work? The colours that make up white light all travel at the same speed. When white light enters a prism or the many slanted layers of a beetle's outer surface, it slows down and separates into beams of coloured light. This happens because different colours of light slow down and bend at different angles.

REFRACTION AND ANGLES

The names applied to refraction are similar to those of reflection. The rays that enter a clear substance, such as glass, are called incident rays. The rays that leave the clear substance are called refracted rays. Rays that hit the clear substance at a right angle are called normal rays.

Here we can see that light rays entering a block of glass, or water, bend towards the normal. This is because glass and water are denser than air and slow down the light rays. When they leave the glass or water and enter air, they bend away from the normal. This happens because air is less dense than water and glass.

▲ Many tropical beetles have a layered outer surface that refracts and reflects light to produce shimmering colours. This helps them blend in with their sunny and leafy environment.

DID YOU KNOW?

▶ When people hunt for fish with spears, they must aim slightly away from the images of the fish they see. By doing so, the hunters allow for the effect of refraction and hopefully catch more fish. This takes a lot of practice. Birds that dive into water to catch fish, such as pelicans (below), have exactly the same problem because they dive after they have seen the fish they want to catch. The refraction of the light means that they do not see exactly where the fish is positioned.

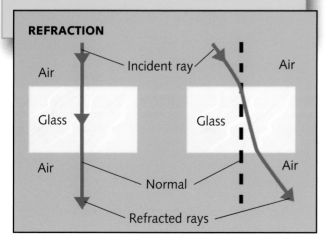

REFRACTION

Air

Incident ray

Air

Glass

Glass

Air

Air

Normal

Refracted rays

Colours

We see a world of colour because objects either transmit (give out), reflect or absorb the colours hidden in white light. This white page reflects all of the colours, so that you see white. These printed words absorb all of the colours so that you see black. The petals of these red flowers (below) reflect red light, but absorb the others, so you see them as red.

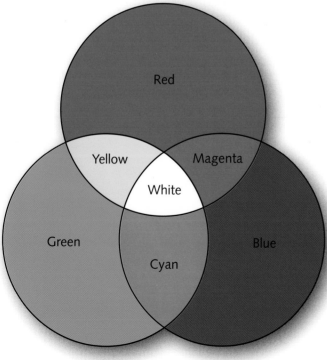

COLOURS OF LIGHT

We know that white light contains the colours of the rainbow. Red, green and blue are the **primary colours of light** because any colour of light can be made from them. Although it may seem surprising, red and green light mix to make yellow when shone onto a white background. Green and blue light make cyan. Red and blue light make magenta. Yellow, cyan and magenta are the secondary colours of light. All three primary colours mix to make white light and the absence of all three makes black.

◀ The primary colours of light are red, green and blue. They mix to make the secondary colours, which are magenta, cyan and yellow.

FILTERS

Stage lighting, disco lights and Christmas tree lights all use filters to produce coloured light. Filters block certain wavelengths, or colours, of light. The colour of the filter is the same colour as the light that comes through it. For example, a green filter only lets green light through and absorbs all of the other colours.

Coloured light can also be obtained by burning particular substances. Matches burn with a yellow flame, and gas from a Bunsen burner burns with a blue flame. The colour of the flame depends on the chemical that is burned. Firework manufacturers have taken advantage of this to create stunning firework displays. By adding specific chemicals to a firework, pyrotechnics can control which colours are seen as the firework

burns. Sodium is added to create yellow sparks, barium creates green sparks and chemicals containing strontium produce bright red sparks. Today, firework displays mark many celebrations, and in the USA, over 100 million kilograms of fireworks are exploded each year.

DID YOU KNOW?

▶ Blue light has a short wavelength – it has more up and down movements than a long wavelength wave for each metre that it travels. When sunlight enters Earth's atmosphere, it collides with tiny air molecules and scatters. Blue short wavelength light hits more molecules and therefore scatters more than the longer light wavelengths, such as yellow and red. This is why the sky looks blue.

▶ When the Sun sets on the horizon, its rays must travel through more of the atmosphere than when the Sun is overhead. Light rays hit so many air molecules that only longer wavelength colours can get through. This is why we have red sunsets.

PRIMARY PIGMENT COLOURS

Coloured pigments behave differently to the colours of light. Coloured pigments reflect some colours of light and absorb others. For example, grass looks green because it contains a pigment that reflects green light waves. It absorbs the other colours of light.

The **primary pigment colours** are different to the primary light colours. Red, yellow and blue are the primary pigment colours. A colour created by mixing two primary colours is called a secondary colour. Orange, green and violet are secondary colours. Colours created by mixing combinations of a primary and a secondary colour are called intermediate-secondary colours. Colours containing combinations of all three primary colours are called tertiary (third) colours. The relationship between the primary, secondary, intermediate-secondary and tertiary colours can be more clearly seen in a colour wheel.

COMPLEMENTARY COLOURS

Look at the third colour wheel and you will see that each colour has an opposite colour. The colours are arranged into pairs – red and green, orange and blue, and yellow and violet. These are pairs of 'complementary colours'. They bring out the best in each other visually. For example, red looks even redder when it is contrasted with green. Yellow and orange look brighter against violet and blue.

Greengrocers often display fruit and vegetables against backgrounds that complement their colours. This makes them more attractive to shoppers. Or they display one type of produce next to another type of produce that complements its colour.

COLOUR WHEELS

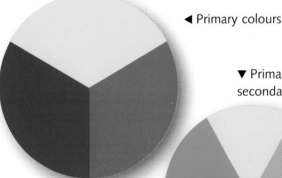

◀ Primary colours

▼ Primary and secondary colours

▼ Primary, secondary and intermediate-secondary colours

▶ These colour wheels show the primary pigment colours, secondary pigment colours (orange, green and violet) the intermediate-secondary colours (yellow-orange, red-orange, red-purple, blue-purple, blue-green and yellow-green) and the tertiary colours (browns, olives, mustards).

▶ Primary, secondary, intermediate-secondary and tertiary colours

If you have some negatives of colour photographs, hold them up to the light and look at them closely. They are called negatives because the colours are reversed. In other words, the colours you see are the complementary colours of those in the actual photograph. The greens and olives of grass and trees will appear as reds and magentas, while the blues and whites of sky and cloud are orange-black, and so on. When the negative is developed, these colours return to their correct appearance.

TONES AND SHADES

The tone of a colour means its lightness or darkness, rather than its actual colour. For example, red comes in many tones – deep red, crimson, scarlet, ruby, red, rose, pink. Each tone includes the same colour but with different amounts of white.

▲ Photographic negatives show the complementary colours of those in the final developed image.

The tones of the things we see around us are due to two things:

> **1.** The amount of light available. The more light is available, the brighter an object looks. The tones in your bedroom look brighter when the Sun is shining through the window than they do on a cloudy day.

> **2.** The overall amount of light reflected and absorbed by an object. Lighter toned objects reflect more light than darker toned objects. Objects that absorb most light and reflect the least are those objects we see as black. You can test this for yourself by placing a sheet of black paper and a sheet of white paper outside on a sunny day. The black paper becomes hotter than the white sheet because it absorbs the Sun's rays.

▲ On a cloudy day, colours can look dull and dark.

Monochrome (single colour) pictures are not just different tones of grey, as in a 'black and white' photograph. They can be tones of any colour. Old photographs from the 1800s are described as 'sepia', and are different tones of brown. They are brown because of the chemicals – egg white, salt and silver nitrate – used to develop the film. The word 'sepia' was originally the name for the brown ink of the cuttlefish. Cuttlefish ink was once used by artists but lost popularity because it fades in sunlight.

▲ On a sunny day, the sunlight makes colours look brighter and more vibrant. The grass looks much 'greener' in the bottom image.

COLOURS IN NATURE

Colours play an important role in nature. Flowers stand out against the background of greens so that many birds and insects visit and pollinate them. Animals themselves are often brightly coloured so that they can be recognised more easily. This is useful when animals are looking for mates, or warning others that they are unpleasant to eat or poisonous. For example, we recognise wasps because of their black and yellow stripes. We know that they sting and so we avoid them. Ladybirds' red and black colouring warns their predators that they taste unpleasant.

In some cases, harmless animals such as hoverflies copy the colours of more dangerous animals such as wasps so that predators will leave them alone. This is called 'mimicry'. In other cases, animals disguise themselves by copying the colours of

things around them, so that predators cannot easily spot them. The fur of an arctic fox is white in the winter and turns brown or grey in the summer to help it hide from predators. This is called 'camouflage'. So, colours can be used to fool enemies and to hide from them.

▲ The colouring of this Arctic fox helps it to hide in the snow covered landscape.

Counter-shading is another protective method of colouration used by many animals, including penguins. Penguins spend a lot of their lives in water. Their dark back feathers help camouflage them from predators that are swimming above them. Their white stomach feathers hide them from predators swimming below.

▲ This harmless hoverfly (above) mimics the colouring of a wasp (right) so that birds think it will sting and so avoid eating it.

Since the Stone Age, over 17,000 years ago, humans have been intrigued by colour. Cave paintings show that early man knew how to make coloured paint by crushing minerals into powder and mixing them with water or animal fats. Stone Age artists used four main colours – black, white, red and yellow. They obtained black from charcoal and manganese ore (a rock found in the Earth). White paint was obtained from clay and limestone-based mud, and red and yellow paint was obtained from animal blood and iron ore.

In the Lascaux cave system in France, archaeologists have identified shells and even a human skull that were used as paint pallets. Painters either rubbed paint onto walls with their fingers, or blew the paint through hollow bird bones. Animals, such as horses and the now extinct woolly rhinoceros, are the most common subject of cave paintings, but some show humans standing next to animals they have killed. Cave paintings are often of excellent quality and have been found right across the world, from Europe to Australia, and the USA to China.

▲ Artists would have worked by primitive oil lights to create beautiful cave paintings.

▼ The paintings at the Lascaux Cave in France show coloured murals of animals and were painted around 17,000 years ago.

▶ Start with paints of the three primary pigment colours – red, yellow and blue – and try to mix the secondary and intermediate-secondary colours found in the third colour wheel on page 22. With practice you'll find that your instincts tell you when you've got each colour about right. Keep a batch of each colour for the next step.

▶ Trace the third colour wheel (page 22) and all twelve segments onto white card. Colour each of the twelve segments with the primary colours and the colours that you have mixed.

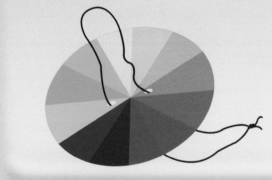

▶ When your colour wheel is dry, cut it out. Pierce the centre twice with a drawing pin. Thread string through one hole, loop it back through the next hole and tie the two ends together. Twist the string and pull it to spin the colour wheel as fast as you can. What happens? The colour wheel looks white because all of the wavelengths of light are reflected. They combine to create white light.

COLOURS AND HUMANS

Colours and patterns can powerfully affect humans, which is why many people enjoy paintings. Scientists have shown that yellows, oranges and reds can make people feel hungry, while blues and purples can put people off eating. For example, many set price 'all you can eat' buffet restaurants choose blue place settings and wall colourings in an attempt to reduce the amount eaten. The restaurant owners hope to save money in this way.

We describe some colours as cool and calming, while other colours are said to be vibrant and exciting. In some countries, red is used to

▶ Colours play a role in religion. In Buddhism, gold is very important. It represents the Sun or fire and has been used since ancient times.

represent anger, which is why we have the saying 'to see red'. Green is often used to describe jealousy or envy, as in 'the green eyed monster'. Blue is associated with sadness, as in 'feeling blue', while yellow describes a coward, as in 'yellow bellied'. The reason behind these uses of colour in language is that we associate their characteristics with moods and emotions. Red is often seen as a warm colour, while blue is cold, for example. However, different cultures attach different meanings to colours. Yellow is a sacred colour to the Chinese, but means sadness in Greece and jealousy in France. In China, white is the colour associated with death, whereas in the UK and the USA, it is black, and in Brazil it is purple.

The scientific reason for our fascination with colour is found in the way we evolved. It started when the ape-like ancestors of humans lived in trees. At that time colour vision was important for things such as, telling edible leaves from poisonous ones, choosing ripe fruits to eat and avoiding dangerous animals. Many rotten foods are blue or black, which may explain why the colour blue is thought to put people off eating. In the past, colour appreciation was a matter of survival. Even today, soldiers use colours to help them survive by wearing green and brown printed uniforms to camouflage themselves against foliage.

▲ Darkly-coloured food is usually off-putting to humans and reduces our appetites. This could be because rotting food eventually darkens and turns purple or black.

▶ Soldiers' uniforms are the same colour as the landscape in which they wish to hide.

TEST YOURSELF

▶ Describe three different colourful organisms and explain how their colour is useful.

5

Seeing the light

Our vision depends on light travelling from an object to our eyes. Our eyes are designed to receive light and our brains can make sense of the light signal. Our brains turn the light signal into images that we understand. We rely on our vision to tell us the shape and colour of an object, how close or far away it is, and whether it is stationary or moving towards or away from us.

SENSING LIGHT

It is estimated that life began on Earth about 3.6 billion years ago. For the first two billion years or so, life was nothing more than very simple organisms called bacteria, which were made from single cells. But then many-celled organisms began to develop. They had to compete for food. Some became hunters, while others became the hunted, and it became necessary to develop senses. The first sense to develop was the sense of touch, which enabled organisms to feel their environments. Then came their ability to taste or sense chemicals. Eventually came sight, which enabled organisms to see by sensing light.

Animals sense light with photoreceptive, or light-receiving, cells. The cells tell the brain that light is present and how bright it is. Sometimes they tell the brain what colour the light is too. In very simple animals these photoreceptive cells tell the brain whether they are in light or darkness. Earthworms, for example, have 'simple eyes' placed along their bodies so that they can tell when they are exposed above the soil and when they are safely below ground.

In more advanced creatures, such as insects, spiders and crabs, the photoreceptive cells are grouped together to form 'compound eyes'. The brain is sent hundreds of individual messages from the cells. It pieces them together to form an image of what the animal is looking at. These eyes provide very good vision, which explains why it is so difficult to swat a fly.

▼ A housefly's two compound eyes each contain about 4,000 separate image-forming structures. Each structure contains a lens and light-sensitive cells.

The most advanced creatures, such as fish, amphibians, reptiles, birds and mammals – including humans – have 'complex eyes'. They have thousands of photoreceptive cells, which form a cup shape at the back of the eye. This is the retina. At the front of the eye is a **lens**. The lens is a transparent disc, which focuses light onto the retina. The brain uses this information to create a very exact picture of the world around the animal. The photoreceptive cells that detect levels of light and dark are called rod cells. Those that detect colour are called cone cells.

A HUMAN EYE

The lens focuses the light onto the retina.

Retina

The cornea covers the front of the eye and helps focus the light.

The iris is the coloured part of the eye. It contracts and expands to open and close the pupil and allow the right amount of light through.

The optic nerve carries information to the brain.

▲ Light enters the eye through the lens and hits the light-sensitive cells of the retina.

The brain works hard to allow us to see the world around us properly. Firstly, it must piece together the thousands of messages sent by our photoreceptive cells and trick our mind so that we see a clear image instead of one made from thousands of dots. Secondly, the image detected by the photoreceptive cells is actually upside down. This is because the lens focuses light in such a way that the beams of light cross over. Our brain flips everything over again so that we see things the right way up. Thirdly, we have two eyes, so our brain has to overlap two sets of information to come up with something that makes sense visually.

MONOCULAR AND BINOCULAR VISION

When an eye works alone it provides **monocular vision**. One eye cannot see depth, so that the image it sees is flat, or two-dimensional (2D). When two eyes work together they provide **binocular vision**. They can judge depth and the image is three-dimensional (3D). Although animals usually have two eyes, some have monocular vision, and others have binocular vision.

▲ A hare's eyes are positioned on each side of its head so that it can see predators approaching from any direction. The eyes work independently and the hare therefore has monocular vision.

Monocular animals are usually prey animals (the hunted). They have two eyes and one eye is found on each side of the animal's head. This enables them to see all around, giving them a better chance of escaping from predators. However, they find it difficult to judge the distance between them and their predators. Rabbits, deer and many fish are monocular animals.

Binocular animals are usually predators (hunters). Both eyes are on the front of their head, as in humans. Predators need binocular vision to see their prey clearly and judge distances exactly, otherwise they wouldn't be as skilled at catching their food. Tree-climbing animals also benefit from binocular vision. It helps them to judge the size of branches and the distances between them, which makes them less likely to make mistakes and injure themselves.

SEEING IN COLOUR

Being able to see in colour is useful when animals need to tell apart edible from non-edible prey. Human eyes are designed so that the photo-receptive cells found in the middle of the retina detect colours very well. The photoreceptive cells around the edge of the retina mainly detect light but not colour. This black and white vision easily detects movement and helps us see better in the dark.

▲ All cats, like this cheetah, have binocular vision to help them judge distances and catch prey.

INVESTIGATE

▶ See for yourself how binocular vision is different to monocular vision. Stretch your arms out straight to the sides at shoulder height. Point your index fingers. Close one eye and bring the tips of your index fingers together in front of you, bending your elbows. Your fingers are likely to miss one another, even though it looks as though they should be exactly in line. That is because you only have monocular vision when one eye is closed. If you try the same experiment again with both eyes open, you'll have no problem because you are using binocular vision.

▶ People have told stories of ghosts throughout history, but as yet, there is no scientific evidence proving that ghosts exist. So how can it be that people see them? Our brains convert lots of pieces of information from our eyes into something that makes sense. It also uses a store of familiar images to recognise things more quickly. Scientists believe that the brain can imagine visual images that appear to come from the eyes, especially when we are tired or frightened. So people do actually see ghosts in front of their eyes, due to the power of suggestion.

COLOUR BLINDNESS

Some animals can't tell the difference between colours – they are colour blind. This isn't because there is anything wrong with them. It is because they don't really need to see colour and by not doing so they are better able to detect movements instead. For this reason many predators, such as dogs and cats, and prey animals, such as rabbits and deer, cannot see colours well. This type of vision is called 'monochromatic' which means 'one coloured'. It is sometimes called 'black and white' vision.

Humans can also be colour blind. Colour blindness is passed on to us from our parents and is much more common in males than in females. Our eyes' cone cells (cells that are sensitive to coloured light) either contain chemicals sensitive to red light, blue light or green light. If one of these types of cone cells is missing then we can't see that particular colour well and may confuse it with a different colour. Around 10 per cent of males and 0.4 per cent of females are colour blind.

▼ This is a test for red-green colour blindness. A person with a red deficiency will only see the orange parts of the eye. Those with a green deficiency will only see the red parts of the eye. A person with normal vision will be able to see green, red and orange, and the complete image of an eye.

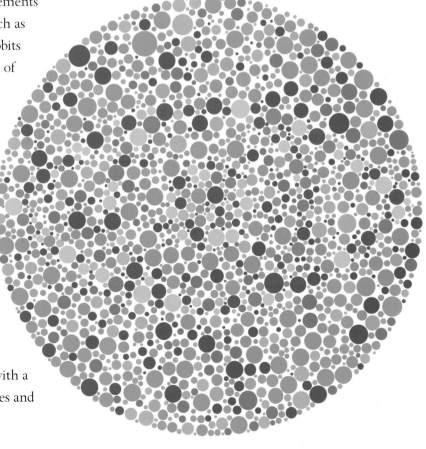

6

The bigger and smaller picture

Human beings have eyesight well suited to tasks that came naturally during evolution, such as hunting, gathering and preparing food, as well as making tools, clothing and shelter. However, when people began to investigate the world in more depth, they found ways to improve their sight. The most important device designed for improving human vision is the artificial lens. An artificial lens is a curved piece of plastic or glass.

Lenses were first used in spectacles in the 1200s. Today we use lenses in spectacles to accurately correct bad eyesight, in microscopes to see objects that are invisible to the naked eye, in telescopes to study stars billions of kilometres from Earth, and in cameras to capture the world around us.

MAGNIFICATION AND CORRECTION

The most basic artificial lens is the magnifying glass (above right). It makes an object look bigger – it magnifies it. For people with good vision, a magnifying glass enables them to study objects or pictures in close-up without straining their eyes. For people with poor eyesight a magnifying glass can correct their sight so that they can see things in focus.

Vision problems such as **long** and **short sightedness** are caused when the lenses in our eyes do not focus light onto the retina. The light still falls on the retina but the image is out of focus. Those with long sight can see clearly far into the distance, but have trouble seeing objects just centimetres away. Short sighted people have the opposite problem. They can clearly see objects right in front of them, but cannot see distant objects clearly.

SIGHT DEFECTS OF THE HUMAN EYE

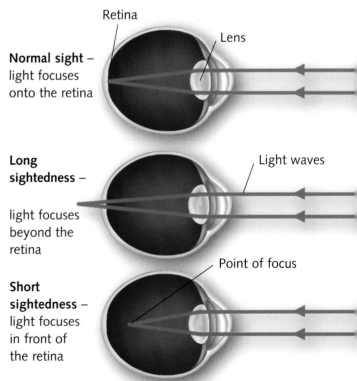

Normal sight – light focuses onto the retina

Long sightedness – light focuses beyond the retina

Short sightedness – light focuses in front of the retina

LASER EYE SURGERY

Ultraviolet laser treatment can be used to correct poor eyesight. The cool laser reshapes the cornea (the outer shell of the eye), so that the eye changes shape very slightly and adjusts the vision of the patient by moving the lens in relation to the retina.

CATARACTS

Sometimes people lose their vision because their lens goes cloudy – a cataract. A simple operation is used to replace the cloudy lens with a plastic one. The only problem is that the plastic lens has a fixed shape, so different pairs of glasses have to be used to focus on things at varying distances.

MICROSCOPES AND TELESCOPES

Around 1600, scientists discovered that an image could look even bigger when two lenses were used instead of one. This led to the invention of both the light microscope and the telescope. There is no real difference between the microscope and telescope, except that microscopes are designed to focus on extremely near objects and telescopes focus on extremely distant objects. They both dramatically magnify the image.

Light microscopes have a series of lenses. The condenser lens focuses light onto the slide to light it up. The objective lens brings the image into focus inside the microscope. The eyepiece lens then magnifies the image further. To get a crystal clear image, the distance between the objective lens and the eyepiece lens is adjusted.

When telescopes involve two lenses they are called refractors because they change the direction of light. They are most useful for looking at distant objects on Earth. For space, a reflector telescope is much more effective. Isaac Newton invented the more powerful reflector telescope in 1670, so that

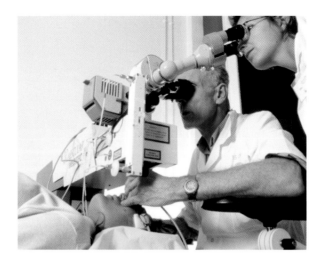

▲ Laser eye surgery can correct eyesight by reshaping the cornea.

he could observe the planets and stars in more detail than the refractor telescope would allow. Reflector telescopes use curved mirrors instead of lenses to collect and focus light.

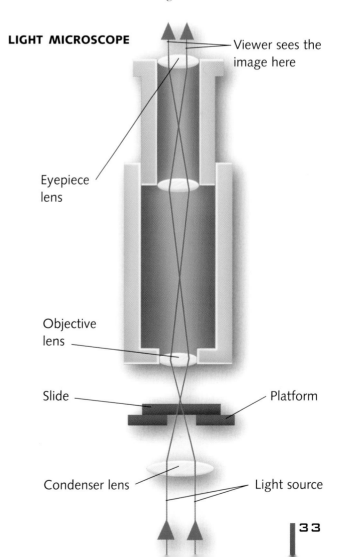

LIGHT MICROSCOPE

Viewer sees the image here

Eyepiece lens

Objective lens

Slide

Platform

Condenser lens

Light source

The Hubble telescope was the world's first space-based telescope. It was sent into orbit around Earth in April 1990 and has been sending back extraordinarily detailed images of stars, planets and galaxies ever since. It is a reflecting telescope and its two mirrors are so smooth that if they were the size of the Earth, the largest bump would be only 15 centimetres high. This reduces the distortion in the final image. Astonishingly, the Hubble telescope can see galaxies that are 10-15 billion light years away.

▼ This deep-field image taken by the Hubble space telescope shows galaxies hundreds of thousands of light years across, and billions of light years away.

INVENTION OF THE CAMERA

Human beings not only want to see clearly; we often want to 'catch and save' moments in time. One of the very first cameras was the camera obscura, which was invented in Italy in the 1500s. A camera obscura projects an image onto a surface, but it does not permanently record the image. If you were in a dark room on a bright day and made a small hole in the window blind or curtain, on the opposite wall there would be an image of the outside world in full colour. The image would even have movement – if a car drives past outside, you would see this in the image. The only difference would be that the image would be upside down. But how does this work? Almost all objects reflect light. Light travels in straight lines. When light rays pass through a small hole in thin material, they cross over and form an upside down image on a surface. To permanently record the image, it must be projected onto light-sensitive film instead. The first photograph was taken using the principle of the camera obscura in the 1850s. The camera was called a pinhole camera. The light-sensitive film can be developed into a photograph.

CAMERA OBSCURA

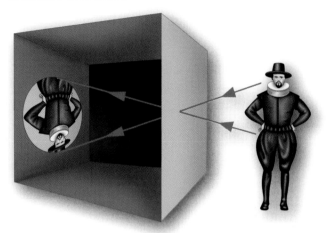

▲ The camera obscura projects real time images onto a surface. The image is always upside down.

INVESTIGATE

▶ To make your own pinhole camera you will need:
One empty can of crisps (or other similar tube with a lid and base) and its lid, duct tape, scissors, a saw, a drawing pin

❶ Clean out the can.
❷ Ask an adult to saw through the can four centimetres from the bottom.
❸ Remove the plastic lid and put it on the shorter half.
❹ Put the longer tube on top of the shorter tube. This should make one long tube with the metal bottom, the lid four centimetres from the bottom and the original opening at the top.
❺ Use duct tape to stick the two tubes together. Then, tape around the entire tube to make sure that no light can enter except through the top.
❻ Make a tiny hole in the metal bottom with a drawing pin.
Take your pinhole camera outside on a bright sunny day and look through the top opening. Cup your hands around the end of the tube that you're looking through to prevent light from entering. What do you see?

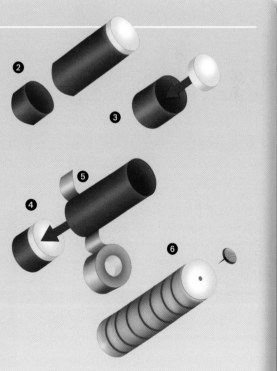

You should see an upside-down and back-to-front-image of the world around you.

CAMERA LUCIDA

The camera lucida was invented in 1807 and was used to copy drawings and paintings. It uses one mirror, instead of a simple hole, to project light reflected by an original artwork onto a second semi-transparent mirror. Skilled artists could see the reflected image and trace it onto a piece of paper. The size of the projected image could be made bigger or smaller. People often had black and white printed copies of famous paintings in their homes, either mounted on their walls or in books, so the camera lucida was a popular invention.

CAMERA LUCIDA

Half silvered glass
(semi-transparent
mirror)

Eye

Object

Mirror

Path of light

Appearance
of object
on paper

CAMERAS WITH LENSES

The first cameras to have lenses were called box cameras. This was for the simple reason that they were nothing more than boxes, with the lens at one end and the photographic film at the other end. The image was brought into focus by moving the lens back and forth. Eventually cameras became more complex and compact, so that they were smaller and easier to use. This also made them cheaper and more popular.

Today there are three basic types of camera – the instamatic ('point and shoot' or 'snapshot'), the SLR (single lens reflex) and the digital camera.

The instamatic's viewfinder (window through which you look) is a simple window through the camera. It does not show the actual image that will be taken through the lens, but it gives the user a rough idea of what will be in the picture.

The SLR is a more professional camera. The user sees through the same lens that the camera uses to capture the image. With instamatic and SLR cameras, the image is recorded onto film, which can be printed onto photo paper.

Digital cameras still use lenses but the image is recorded by an in-built computer instead of onto film.

▲ Digital cameras have a screen onto which the image is projected. The images must be downloaded to a computer, or a photo printer, and then printed.

▲ ▶ Movie cameras capture images onto spools of film.

MOVIE CAMERAS

Movie cameras are similar to ordinary cameras.
They capture a series of still images onto spools
of film. The films are then processed and
projected quickly one after the other to give
the illusion of movement.

Television cameras, video cameras and digital
cameras capture their images in a similar way, but
the sequences of pictures are recorded and
displayed differently. All moving images work by
deceiving the eye so that it 'sees' a continual
image in motion. For a realistic and smooth sense
of movement the eye needs about 24 separate
images every second. That's 1440 images per
minute, or 86,400 every hour!

INVESTIGATE

▶ Find out and explain what the term 'exposure'
means in relation to light and photography.

7

The light fantastic

Light is something most of us take for granted because it is a normal part of our world. It is not only responsible for our survival; it has many unusual uses, too. It carries our voices along telephone cables, reads CDs, DVDs and barcodes, tricks the eye into seeing things that aren't really there, and breaks down plastics.

Light exits the cable.

FIBRE OPTIC CABLE

Light enters the cable.

FIBRE OPTICS

Light is reflected by shiny surfaces. Light can travel along thin glass or plastic rods and emerge at the other end by bouncing off the reflective internal surface. These rods are called fibre optics. They are used to channel light around corners and over long distances. When we speak into a landline telephone, the information is changed from sound into flashing lights. This works as a code. The receiving phone decodes the series of flashes and turns it into sound again. More information can be sent by light than it can by electrical signals because electrical signals heat the wire and lose energy. Light signals do not lose as much energy and the information remains clearer.

Path of light through cable

▲ The inside walls of a fibre optic cable reflect light. All the light that enters the fibre at one end, leaves at the other end.

LIGHT THERAPY

Human beings are suited to the daily cycle of light and darkness. In fact, our biological systems work on a 24-hour clock, called our 'circadian rhythm'. Our bodies and minds are affected by our sense of vision, because it tells us whether it is daytime or night time.

Sometimes our circadian rhythm can be upset by changes in our routine, so that we have trouble sleeping, staying awake or feeling happy. This can happen when people do shift work, if they travel long distances by air, or when the days grow shorter in winter. However, it has been discovered that we can fool our minds and bodies with the use of light boxes, which our bodies respond to as if they are daylight. Light boxes contain fluorescent light tubes behind a white screen. They can re-set our circadian rhythms and improve our moods and sleep patterns. Patients sit in front of the box for 10 to 45 minutes a day and most people notice an improvement in just a few days.

▲ Light boxes are used to re-set people's circadian rhythms.

LIGHT AND THE ENVIRONMENT

Some modern plastics react to light. Photo-degradable plastics become brittle and break down in the presence of sunlight. They can be used to make plastic carrier bags and ringed can carriers. This reduces the volume of litter in the environment and helps prevent harm to wildlife. Photodegradable plastic ringed can carriers, which can get caught around the necks of animals, lose 75 per cent of their strength when exposed to sunlight for a few days. After a few weeks, they completely disintegrate. Ordinary plastic can take between 15 and 1,000 years to break down.

▲ Ordinary plastic ringed can carriers are eaten by birds or can get stuck around a bird's neck. In this way, plastic rubbish can kill wildlife.

DENTISTS AND LIGHT

Some materials harden when they are exposed to light. Any material that does this is described as 'photosetting'. You may have one or more fillings in your teeth. Fillings used to be a dark silver colour, but today dentists often use white fillings called 'composite resin fillings'. These are far less obvious than traditional fillings. Once the dentist has filled your tooth, he shines ultraviolet light on the resin. This hardens it and prevents decay from eating away at your tooth.

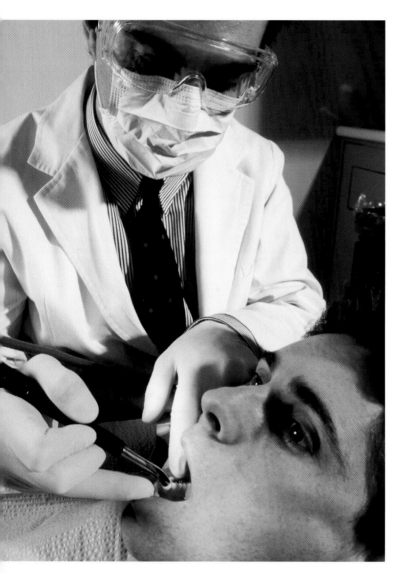

▲ Dentists use light to make the white fillings in your teeth set hard.

CDs AND DVDs

Playing music and movies on CDs (compact discs) and DVDs (digital video discs) involves the use of laser light. The information is stored on the disc in the form of a line, which spirals from the inside to the outside edge. It has a code made from tiny pits in the surface. These pits are read by the laser beam, which detects whether or not a pit is present, and how long or short it is. Several million pits pass the laser beam every minute and the information is decoded to create sounds and images. These discs reflect light in the colours of the spectrum because white light refracts in the pits, in the same way that raindrops in the sky form a rainbow effect through refraction.

▼ These pits on the surface of a CD or DVD have been magnified around 3,450 times.

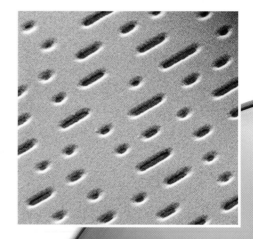

CHECKOUT SCANNERS

Barcode scanners at supermarket checkouts also use laser light. This time, instead of reading pits, the light beam reads the bands of black and white that make up a barcode. White reflects light while black does not. So, the scanner reads the amount of light reflected and this tells it the distance between and width of the white parts. This forms a code, which a computer in the till reads to find out the cost of the product.

▲ Barcodes are used on almost all items sold in shops. They are a simple way of creating a universal code by which a product can be recognised.

There are two types of scanner. The clever ones can read a barcode from different angles. They are usually found under a desk, where a spinning disk scatters the laser light in many directions to find the barcode. The hand-held scanners pulse the laser left to right over the barcode. Laser beams are very useful for this purpose because they are very precise and can be easily turned on and off.

▼ Barcodes are read by laser lights in scanners.

HOLOGRAMS

Holograms are artificially produced pictures that fool the eye into seeing 3D objects. 3D images not only have width and height (two dimensions), they also have depth. Your eyes are roughly five centimetres apart and the view from each eye is slightly different. Our brains overlap these two images to create a 3D image. Holograms try to re-create this artificially. There are several different types of hologram.

(2) The 3D film. Each scene is filmed from two viewpoints. Both are projected onto the cinema screen at once – one in red, and one in blue or green. For this to work, the viewer wears special viewing glasses. The coloured filters in the glasses separate the two images so that each image only enters one eye. Your brain puts the images back together and you see the film in 3D. Watching a 3D film without the glasses is a very strange sight and looks as though you are seeing double!

(3) Transmission holograms. You don't need to wear viewing glasses to see these holograms. Firstly, a laser light is used to create a 3D pattern of the subject, such as a statue, on a glass plate. Secondly, a laser light is scattered and reflected by the pattern to generate dots of light in the air. These make up a 3D image of the statue that looks so real that you want to reach out and touch it, which of course is impossible.

▲ This tiny figure is a hologram made from laser light. It is a transmission hologram.

(1) The simplest holograms are made from layers of clear plastic filters with grooves in the surface. The grooves reflect light at different angles to make sure that each of our eyes receives a slightly different version of the image underneath. These are the holograms used on bubblegum cards.

(4) Reflection holograms. These holograms are often found on credit cards because they are very difficult to forge. They are created by a complicated process, which involves shining laser lights onto the subject, such as an apple, and onto a photographic film. This records patterns of light and dark on the film, which make up the 3D hologram. Ordinary light is shone onto the film and we see an image that looks almost exactly like the original subject.

TIME TRAVEL: INTO THE FUTURE

Holography is not just used to store images. It can also be used to store data. A music CD (right) can hold about 700 MB (or 0.7 GB) of data, which is around 75 minutes of music. A double-sided, double-layered DVD can hold around 15.9 GB of data.

Scientists are always looking for ways to store more and more data. One way of doing this may be holographic memory. Instead of just storing information on the surface of an object, information would also be stored beneath the surface. A sugar cube sized crystal of holographic memory could store 1,000 GB of data.

Laser light can be used to create holographic memory devices. Two laser beams create a pattern, or code, inside a light-sensitive crystal. Each page of data is stored in a different area of the crystal. Then, by firing a laser at the crystal at exactly the same angle as the original laser, the coded data can be retrieved. The data is interpreted by a machine called a charge-couple device camera, and is sent to a computer.

Holographic memory could be with us by 2007, although some scientists are less optimistic and feel that it still needs considerable development. In the next five to ten years, we will either all be using holographic memory, or it will commercially be a complete flop. We will just have to wait and see.

VIRTUAL REALITY

Over the last 20 years, a great deal of time, money and effort has been put into developing virtual reality systems. Virtual reality systems create the impression of a real experience, but in a safe environment. Flight simulators, for example, use visual information to make a trainee pilot feel as though the experience is real. That way, the pilot can learn how to fly effectively, but it doesn't matter if he or she crashes the virtual aircraft. Virtual reality helmets provide each eye with a slightly different image, just as holograms do, so that the person 'sees' a very convincing 3D virtual world. Most systems are used for playing games, but learning and playing are very similar processes for the human brain.

▶ At a NASA research centre, this virtual reality helmet and glove are used to control a robot.

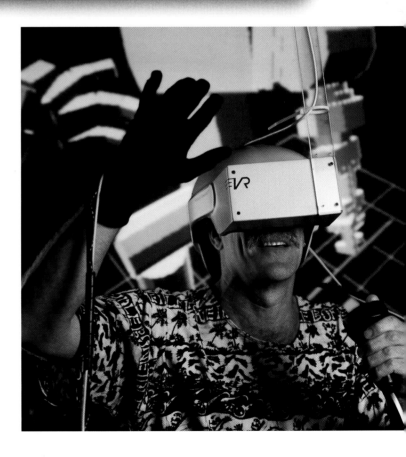

HEAT HAZES AND MIRAGES

Sometimes when you drive along a straight road on a hot day it is possible to see something known as a 'heat haze'. Hot air rises from the tarmac and causes ripples that give the appearance of water. The ripples appear because hot air mixes with cooler air above it and this moving air refracts the rays of light.

In its most extreme form, a heat haze can create an optical illusion called a mirage. They occur in very hot places, such as deserts. People think they can see things that aren't there – lakes, forests and even cities. What they are often seeing is the reflected and then refracted light from real objects, which are actually much farther away.

The light is reflected from the real object and then gets bounced along, rather like a giant optical fibre, until it enters the person's eyes. Mirages can appear to be so real that people have been known to walk towards them for hours, without ever arriving.

TEST YOURSELF

▶ Light is important to life on Earth for many reasons. Can you think of five ways in which light has affected you today?

▼ Heat hazes are caused by the refraction of light rays through hot, rising air. This often looks like water.

TIME TRAVEL: INTO THE FUTURE

Scientists may have found a way to begin developing a real life 'holodeck' as seen in the science fiction show, Star Trek. The idea of the 'holodeck' is that an environment is simulated electronically so that people see a hologram as if it were real, without wearing any special apparatus. Scientists have shown that particles of matter can be held in place by the light beams of a hologram, which they've dubbed 'holographic tweezers'. So it might be possible to build a whole three-dimensional illusion from particles, rather like a stage set.

Space agencies across the world are investigating powering spacecraft with sunlight. Light is a form of energy and scientists believe sunlight could be used to propel rockets once they are in space. The sunlight pushes on the spacecraft's solar sails and could eventually push the craft at over 240 kilometres per hour.

Scientists at the University of Florida have genetically engineered plants so that they make a protein that will glow green if they are not happy with their surroundings. Scientists have put a gene into the plants which causes them to glow with fluorescent light. The idea is that they will glow when under stress. For example, some plants could glow if there is not enough water, and others could glow if the quality of the soil is poor. NASA hopes to send the seeds of such plants to Mars to be grown in Martian soil in specially-designed greenhouses. Cameras would monitor the plants and the telltale glows would be relayed back to Earth, indicating when something wasn't right. Seeds that thrive would not glow at all. NASA hopes that the first plants will be on Mars within a decade and that this will pave the way for humans to eventually live on Mars.

▼ The plants on the left have been photographed in normal light. The plants on the right have been photographed in short wave blue light and are giving off the telltale glow.

Glossary

BINOCULAR VISION – This is when an organism's two eyes work together. The image from each eye is blended together by the brain to produce a complete image in which the organism can detect depth. Animals with binocular vision usually have both eyes positioned on the front of their heads.

BIOLUMINESCENCE – The production of light by a chemical reaction in living organisms, such as some insects, plankton and fish.

COHERENCE – When the peaks and troughs of light waves are all lined up they are said to be coherent. Laser light is coherent light.

DIFFUSION – This is when light waves are scattered in many different directions. For example, frosted glasses diffuses light.

ECLIPSE – In space, when one object moves into the shadow of another object, an eclipse has occurred. A solar eclipse is when the Moon is positioned between the Sun and the Earth. The Earth is then in the Moon's shadow.

INCANDESCENT LIGHT – Light given out by a hot object.

IRIDESCENCE – Gleaming colours caused by the refraction of light.

LENS – A transparent object that focuses light in spectacles, microscopes, telescopes and in the eye.

LONG SIGHT – A vision defect in which light is focussed beyond the retina at the back of the eye. Long-sighted people cannot clearly see near objects.

LUMINESCENT LIGHT – Light given out by an object which does not involve heat.

LUMINOUS – An object that emits light.

MASS – The amount of matter within an object.

MONOCULAR VISION – This is when an organism's eyes work independently. The image from each eye does not overlap and as a result such organisms have difficulty detecting depth. Animals with monocular vision have their eyes positioned on the sides of their heads.

NON-LUMINOUS – An object that does not emit light.

ANSWERS

P8 Investigate
A lunar eclipse happens when the Sun, Earth and Moon line up in that order. The Moon passes through the Earth's shadow. A lunar eclipse only happens at full Moon.

It is dangerous to look directly at the Sun because the Sun's rays can burn the cells of the retina. This can cause permanent vision damage.

P11 Test yourself
As you move an object closer to an artificial light source, the object blocks more and more light waves. This is because the light waves radiate out from a central point. Therefore, as more light waves are blocked, the shadow grows larger.

With sunlight, the size of the shadow remains the same. This is because the Sun is so distant from the Earth, that by the time the light waves reach Earth they are travelling more or less parallel. As you move an object, the distance between the Sun and the object changes only very slightly compared to the great distance from the Earth to the Sun. This change is not enough to block significantly more or fewer light waves and the shadow stays the same size.

Richard Of York Gave Battle In Vain

P18 Investigate
It takes two mirrors to see the back of your head. Stand with your back to a wall mirror. Hold a second mirror in your right hand so that

it is just in front and to the right of your head. Look in the hand-held mirror and position it so that you can see your reflection in the wall mirror. You can also see the back of your head if you stand in the same position and hold the hand-held mirror in your left hand. Hold it to the left of your head and see the reflection of the back of your head in the wall mirror.

P26 Investigate
The colour wheel looks white because all of the wavelengths of light are reflected. They combine and you see the wheel as white.

P27 Test yourself
Colourful snakes – This kind of colouring sends a message to other animals warning them to stay away. The other animals will know through

OPAQUE – A material or substance that does not allow light to travel through it.

PHOSPHORESCENCE – This is when an object absorbs light energy and then slowly releases it again over a period of time. Phosphorescent paint is used on glow-in-the-dark objects.

PRIMARY COLOURS OF LIGHT – Three colours of light that when mixed together make white light. The colours are red, green and blue.

PRIMARY PIGMENT COLOURS – Colours that can not be made from any other colours. They are red, yellow and blue.

RADIATION – Energy that is transmitted from a source in the form of rays, waves or particles. Visible light, heat and x-rays are all different kinds of radiation.

REFLECT – To bounce back from a surface. The surface of a mirror reflects almost all of the light that hits it.

SHORT SIGHT – A vision defect in which light is focussed in front of the retina which itself is located at the back of the eye. Short-sighted people cannot clearly see distant objects.

SPEED OF LIGHT – The speed at which light travels through a vacuum (a space with nothing in it). This is around 300,000 kilometres per second.

TRANSLUCENT – A material that is partially transparent. It allows some light to pass through, but images cannot be clearly seen through translucent materials.

TRANSPARENT – A material that lets virtually all light pass through it. Clear glass is transparent. Images can be clearly seen through transparent materials.

WAVELENGTH – The distance from the crest of one wave to the crest of the next wave.

Useful websites:

www.bbc.co.uk/schools
www.howstuffworks.com
www.newscientist.com
www.popsci.com
www.sciencenewsforkids.org

---

either instinct or from a previous experience that the colourful snake may harm them.

Rabbits – Wild rabbits are usually brown, which makes them less noticeable to predators. When they are alarmed and run for cover, their white tails flash a warning signal to the other rabbits.

Birds – The bright colours of a male bird's feathers attract female birds in preparation for mating.

P30 Investigate
This experiment demonstrates that the use of one eye on its own – monocular vision – results in an inability to detect depth. When two eyes are used together – binocular vision – depth detection is far better.

P35 Investigate
We see objects because they reflect light. Your pinhole camera allows light to enter through a tiny hole. The light has come from the object at which you are pointing the camera. The light waves hit the plastic lid and the coloured and reflected light forms an image on the lid. The image is upside-down and back-to-front because the light waves cross over as they pass through the pinhole.

P37 Investigate
In relation to light and photography, the term 'exposure' refers to the amount of time that the light-sensitive film is exposed to light. When photographing fast-moving objects, such as a runner, the exposure time should be short. This prevents blurring. When it is dark, the exposure time needs to be longer so that enough light hits the sensitive film to record the image.

P44 Test yourself
(1) Light is vital to make plants grow. Plants provided me with oxygen gas and food.

(2) Light allowed me to speak to someone in a different town because landline telephones work using light signals.

(3) Light helped me to see to find my way to school.

(4) Coloured traffic lights prevented accidents.

(5) Light is important to help keep my skin healthy.

Index

Page references in italics
represent pictures.

PHOTO CREDITS – (abbv: r, right, l, left, t, top, m, middle, b, bottom) **Cover background image** Royalty-Free/Corbis **Front cover images** (r) www.istockphoto.com/Michael Renner (l) www.istockphoto.com/Tracie Jibbens **Back cover image** (inset) www.istockphoto.com/Michael Renner **p.1** (tr) www.istockphoto.com/Mark Kalkwarf (bl) www.istockphoto.com/Tom Marvin (br) Raymond Blythe/Oxford Scientific **p.2** www.istockphoto.com/Brian Stanback **p.2-3** www.istockphoto.com/Don Wilkie **p.3** (tr) www.istockphoto.com/Holger Ehlers (br) www.istockphoto.com/Justin Horrocks **p.4** (tr) www.istockphoto.com/Mark Strozier (tl) www.istockphoto.com/Olga Drozdova (br) www.istockphoto.com/Martin Molenkamp **p.5** NASA, ESA and A. Nota (STScI/ESA) **p.7** www.istockphoto.com/Christopher Messer **p.8** The Living Earth **p.9** David Parker/Science Photo Library **p.10** NASA, ESA and A. Nota (STScI/ESA) **p.11** (tr) www.istockphoto.com/Nancy Louie (bl) David A. Hardy/Science Photo Library **p.12** (t) www.istockphoto.com/Martin Molenkamp (b) www.istockphoto.com/George Cairns **p.13** (t) Raymond Blythe/Oxford Scientific (b) Dick Rowan/Science Photo Library **p.14** (t) James Pomerantz/Corbis (m) Lawrence Lawry/Science Photo Library **p.15** www.istockphoto.com/James McQuillan **p.15** Antonia Reeve/Science Photo Library **p.17** Chris Sattleberger/Science Photo Library **p.18** (t) www.istockphoto.com/Oleg Prikhodko (b) www.istockphoto.com/Olga Drozdova **p.19** (t) www.istockphoto.com/Mark Strozier (b) William Ervin/Science Photo Library **p.20** www.istockphoto.com/Justin Horrocks **p.21** (l) www.istockphoto.com/Mark Kalkwarf (r) www.istockphoto.com/Tom Marvin **p.23** (t) www.istockphoto.com/Don Wilkie (m&b) Simon Morse **p.24** (t) Doug Allan/Science Photo Library (bl) www.istockphoto.com/Laurie Knight (br) www.istockphoto.com/Randy Plett **p.25** (t) Christian Jegou, Publiphoto Diffusion/Science Photo Library (b) Pascal Goetgheluck/Science Photo Library **p.26** www.istockphoto.com/Leeman **p.27** (t) www.istockphoto.com/Jacques Croizer (b) Roy Morsch/Corbis **p.28** Andrew Syred/Science Photo Library **p.29** www.istockphoto.com/Greg Henry **p.30** www.istockphoto.com/Holger Ehlers **p.31** (t) www.istockphoto.com/George Cairns (b) David Nicholls/Science Photo Library **p.32** Pascal Goetgheluck/Science Photo Library **p.33** Bsip Laurent/Science Photo Library **p.34** NASA, ESA, J. Blakeslee and H. Ford (Johns Hopkins University) **p.36** www.istockphoto.com/Lee Pettet **p.37** (t) Douglas Kirkland/Corbis (b) www.istockphoto.com/Andre Maritz **p.38** www.istockphoto.com/Brian Stanback **p.39** (l) Bsip, Laurent/Laeticia/Science Photo Library (r) Joe McDonald/Corbis **p.40** (l) Phototake Inc/Oxford Scientific (m) Andrew Syred/Science Photo Library (br) www.istockphoto.com/Don Wilkie **p.41** (t) www.istockphoto.com/Andrzej Tokarski (b) William Whitehurst/Corbis **p.42** Philippe Plailly/Science Photo Library **p.43** (t) Royalty-Free/Corbis (b) Roger Ressmeyer/Corbis **p.44** Damien Lovegrove/Science Photo Library **p.45** Courtesy Dr. Anna-Lisa Paul and Dr. Robert J. Ferl, Department of Horticultural Sciences, University of Florida.